21st Century Skills Library

POWER UP!
SEARCHING FOR OIL

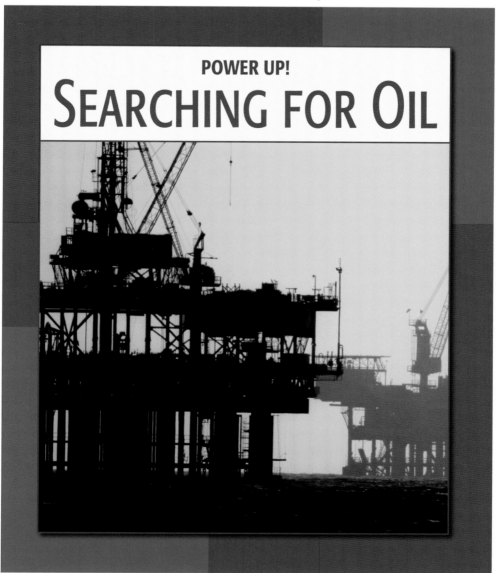

Kathleen Manatt

Cherry Lake Publishing
Ann Arbor, Michigan

Published in the United States of America by Cherry Lake Publishing
Ann Arbor, MI
www.cherrylakepublishing.com

Photo Credits: Page 9, © Photo Courtesy of Library of Congress; Page 18, © CORBIS;
Page 22, © Owen Franken/CORBIS; Page 26, © Jacques Langevin/CORBIS SYGMA

Library of Congress Cataloging-in-Publication Data
Manatt, Kathleen G.
  Searching for oil/by Kathleen Manatt.
     p. cm.— (Power up!)
  ISBN-13: 978-1-60279-043-8 (lib. bdg.)   978-1-60279-100-8 (pbk.)
  ISBN-10: 1-60279-043-4 (lib. bdg.)   1-60279-100-7 (pbk.)
  1. Petroleum—Juvenile literature. 2. Oil well drilling—Juvenile
literature. I. Title. II. Series.
  TN870.3.M36 2008
  553.2'82—dc22   2007006338

*Cherry Lake Publishing would like to acknowledge the work of
The Partnership for 21st Century Skills.
Please visit* www.21stcenturyskills.org *for more information.*

TABLE OF CONTENTS

CHAPTER 1

Energy from Long Ago   4

CHAPTER 2

Where Oil Is Found   11

CHAPTER 3

Locating Oil   14

CHAPTER 4

Drill, Drill, Drill   18

CHAPTER 5

Are We Running Low?   22

Glossary   30

For More Information   31

Index   32

CHAPTER ONE

ENERGY FROM LONG AGO

Every day millions of Americans drive cars and trucks that use gasoline and oil.

Oil! We all use it. It makes our cars, planes, buses, and trucks run.

It heats many homes. It forms the basis for the plastics in our TVs,

computers, blenders, drinking straws, and credit cards. Without oil, our

lives would be very different from what they are.

But what is oil? What is it made of, and how do we find it? These are just some of the questions this book will answer.

Energy is the power to do work. The human body gets energy from food and other nutritional sources. We also need energy to run our machines. Over time we have found or developed many sources of energy. One of the most important sources is oil.

Oil is a **fossil fuel**. It is made from plants and animals that lived millions and millions of years ago. After they died, they slowly became covered with dust, dirt, twigs, and other dead plants and animals. Millions of years went by, and more and more

Fossil fuels are classified as nonrenewable resources, which means once they are used, they cannot easily be replaced. Consider how fossil fuels are created. Why are they classified as nonrenewable?

sediment built up. So did the pressure on the decaying remains. Everything became buried deep in the Earth. Over a long, long time, the decayed remains changed into a gooey, sticky liquid.

In the Past

People have known the value of oil for a long time. Around 400 A.D., people in China were actually drilling oil wells. They used the oil to heat

For more than a thousand years, people have known that oil burns – providing light and heat.

salt water to get the salt itself. By 800 A.D., the Japanese called oil "burning water" and used it for heating and lighting.

Edwin Drake drilled the first oil well in the United States in 1859. It was near Titusville, Pennsylvania. Soon the country was producing more than 125 million barrels a year! At that time oil was used mostly for burning in oil lamps. Oil lamps and candles were the main way to light up the night then.

The first widespread use of oil was for lanterns and lamps. Together with candles, they were the main light sources for centuries.

Internal combustion engines did not power the first cars. The Stanley Steamer, powered by steam from a boiler, was introduced in 1898. However, these cars were not as convenient as those with internal combustion engines. The cars had a top speed of about 35 miles an hour, and drivers had to stop every 20 miles to fill up with water. Why would these be problems on most trips?

Soon big deposits of oil also were found in Russia, Canada, and Mexico. In the United States searchers discovered deposits in Texas, California, and Oklahoma.

And in the early 1900s, what was all this oil being used for? The answer is just one word: cars. The internal combustion engine used in cars runs on gasoline. Gasoline comes from oil.

As more and more people bought cars, the need for oil skyrocketed. Oil became the way to riches. It created the world's first billionaire: John D. Rockefeller. His company, Standard Oil, **refined** oil into gasoline and other products. Founded

8

John D. Rockefeller controlled the oil business in the U.S.
for more than 40 years. He used much of his money to
fund medical research and education.

in 1870, Standard Oil became a **monopoly,** controlling oil refining. In 1911

the U.S. Supreme Court broke Standard Oil into 34 new oil companies.

As the need for oil increased, searching for oil became big business. All kinds of new companies arose. Some drilled for oil. Others made the drilling tools. Some companies collected the oil or built the pipelines to move the oil to ships and trucks. Oil refiners such as Standard Oil processed the **crude oil** into gasoline and other products. Then gas stations began to appear in cities and towns everywhere to sell the gasoline to drivers.

CHAPTER TWO

WHERE OIL IS FOUND

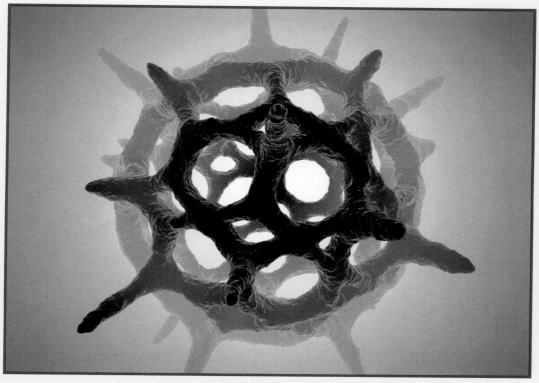

The bodies of millions and millions of tiny plankton, shown here through a microscope, formed the material that turned into petroleum.

Most oil formed at the bottom of ancient seas, lakes, and oceans. It

was in these waters that microscopic animals and plants lived, died, and

fell to the bottom. Over millions of years, pressure and underground heat

"cooked" them and turned them into **petroleum,** or oil, and natural gas. The tiny drops of oil were trapped in **permeable** rocks.

What kinds of rocks are permeable? Sandstone is one kind. It often has many large and well-connected

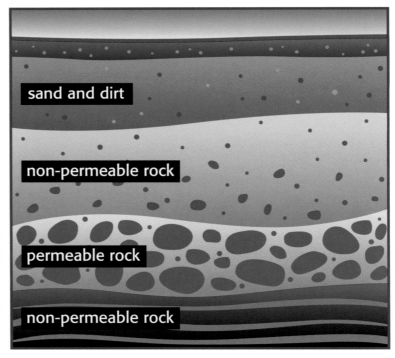

The holes in the permeable rock collected the oil, trapping it between layers of non-permeable rocks. Drilling must pierce the hard rocks above to reach the oil.

pores, or holes. Even though a rock looks solid, if you put it under a microscope, you will see that there are tiny holes in it. If the tiny pores are connected to each other, the rock is permeable. Above these were non-permeable rocks, and below was heavier salt water.

The oil was sometimes forced out of the rocks where it was formed. Slowly, slowly, slowly, some of it oozed through cracks and headed upward, to the Earth's surface. There it sat as pools of tar. The rest is history. People discovered the pools, experimented with the tar, and found it burned well. A new source of energy had been discovered.

The people who found the tar pits probably didn't think about what they found in any step-by-step way. However, today scientists have a method for thinking and testing things. What are some of the steps you would use to figure out how to use something new?

CHAPTER THREE

LOCATING OIL

*The Earth holds big deposits of oil deep in rocks. The trick is
finding it and pumping it to the surface.*

People want and need oil. But how do we find it when it is buried deep

underground? Usually, this is the work of **geologists**. These are people with special college training who study Earth and its internal workings. To

find oil deposits, geologists study satellite photos. They also use tools that

measure tiny, tiny changes in Earth's gravity and magnetic fields.

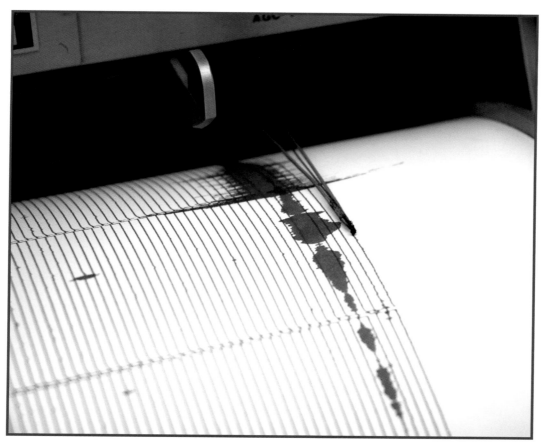

Readings by sensitive instruments tell geologists where they might
find oil. Different kinds of rock give different measurements that
scientists read like a map to the oil reserves.

And often they use thumper trucks. These huge machines bounce up and down on the ground. The vibrations they make are recorded by electrical instruments and turned into special maps. The maps help geologists figure out where oil might be buried.

Thumper trucks are fine for land, but what about oil trapped under the oceans or ice? Geologists may travel on special ships to places in the ocean where oil might be found. First, the ships lay out cables with many listening devices. Then the ships fire air guns into the water and map the results. The maps, like those from thumper trucks, show possible oil deposits.

Once scientists think they have found oil, a "test well" is drilled. A special **drill bit** brings up rock samples. Then the samples are carefully studied to determine if oil is present. Often the answer is no. Even though a great deal of expense has been wasted, oil is so valuable that it is worth it. As a result, when oil is discovered, everybody is very, very happy.

21st Century Content

Oil field technology is one area of business that knows no borders. Because finding oil is so important to so many countries, new techniques are sold or shared with companies or governments around the world.

CHAPTER FOUR

DRILL, DRILL, DRILL

In th 1920s, more than 100 oil wells covered Signal Hill, near Long Beach, California. One of the most productive oil fields in the world became known as "Porcupine Hill".

Once oil has been discovered, the work has just begun. Experts will

study all the evidence to decide exactly where to drill the oil wells to get the

maximum amount of oil out of the ground. They must decide how close together the wells should be. They must determine how many wells to drill. They must also decide how fast the wells should pump. Remember, the oil must flow through tiny, tiny spaces in the rocks.

Drilling for oil also involves a lot of legal work. If the oil well is to be drilled on land, somebody owns the land and will probably want part of any profits. If oil is discovered under the ocean, nearby nations will consider it to be their property. In both cases, contracts will need to be worked out before drilling can legally begin. Drilling wells without the proper contracts will only cause many problems later on.

21st Century Content

Oil deposits were trapped under the ground long before today's countries existed. Now some countries have large deposits below their land, such as Saudi Arabia, Venezuela, and Nigeria, and other countries have few or none. This makes oil a major component of world trade.

Setting up the oil well takes hard work and lots of machinery. The workers on rigs such as this one are called "roughnecks."

Drilling an oil well takes a lot of work. The crew first digs a big circular

ditch around where the well will be. This provides room for the workers

and their tools. The huge oil derrick is delivered on a truck or even with a helicopter. Once drilling begins, water and mud are forced down the sides of the hole to bring up the rock fragments that are being created by the drill bit.

As drilling progresses, more segments of pipe are added. Once the specified depth is reached, core samples are checked. Then a device called a "Christmas tree" is attached to the well at ground level and cemented in place. This device controls the flow of oil from the well.

Now the oil derrick can be taken to another drilling site. It will be replaced with a pump on the wellhead.

CHAPTER FIVE

ARE WE RUNNING LOW?

Many Americans remember the oil shortages of 1973–1974. In reaction to world events, many of the oil-producing countries in the Middle East cut oil sales and raised prices. Gasoline was rationed, meaning people could buy only limited amounts, and the U.S. economy was hurt.

Oil is a **nonrenewable resource**. Once we use it up, there won't be any more for millions and millions of years. During the 1900s, we used oil for just about anything we could think of. By the late 1900s, scientists and others were trying to figure out just how much oil we have left. However, it is difficult to determine how much is left, and the answers vary widely.

Part of the problem is deciding what oil is worth drilling for. Sometimes, oil is buried so deep in the ground that it would cost far too much to get to it. At least that's true for now. As oil becomes scarce, maybe drilling for these hard-to-reach deposits will be

21st Century Content

Although much of the Middle East is now desert, it has a large percentage of the world's oil supply. Countries who use large amounts of oil, such as the United States and Great Britain, keep a close eye on events in the region. Any threat to the oil supply is a very serious matter.

Large oil fields under the sea require massive structures such as this offshore oil rig. In the United States, many platforms dot the Gulf of Mexico and the water around Alaska.

worth it. Even in the United States, some small wells that were once unprofitable were reopened when oil prices went up.

The way each country figures its remaining oil reserves is also confusing. For example, the nation of Abu Dhabi has said its oil **reserves** are 92.3 billion barrels every year since 1988. However, the country has pumped more than 14 billion barrels since then.

Also in 1988, four Middle Eastern

nations more than doubled their estimated reserves.

What's going on here? These nations depend so

heavily on oil income that they may not want to

admit their supplies are decreasing.

Despite disagreement about which country has

how much oil left, everybody agrees we need more.

One promising source is around Fort McMurray,

in the Canadian province of Alberta. The area has a

type of rock called tar sands. This is a combination

of semi-solid crude oil, clay, minerals, and water. And

there's a lot of it! However, getting to this oil greatly

damages the land. Two tons of tar sands yield only

one barrel of oil.

Winters in Fort McMurray are cold. Temperatures can dip to −40 degrees. Why do you think people would be willing to live and work in such a climate?

This tiny bird has been rescued from an oil spill. Most of the birds and sea life die as a result of the spills.

The location of oil deposits has caused an environmental problem. Crude oil and finished products are shipped across the oceans in huge tankers. Sometimes, these tankers have accidents, as the Exxon Valdez did in 1989. Resulting oil spills harm the birds, sea life, and animals for hundreds of miles around the spill. And the spills are very hard to clean up.

Because oil is a nonrenewable resource, we need to find ways to make better use of what we have left. One way is to drive more fuel-efficient vehicles, such as hybrid cars. A government plan to cut oil use in vehicles by 20 percent in a decade would save 550,000 barrels of oil a day. We may also use more gasoline that is partly made up of a fuel called **ethanol**. Ethanol is a fuel made from corn and other grains. This will also cut oil use.

21st Century Content

Brazil is the world leader in ethanol use. All gasoline in Brazil contains at least 20 percent ethanol and almost half the cars use only ethanol as fuel. The United States is following Brazil's lead. There are more than 100 ethanol refineries and construction plans for another fifty or so.

Ethanol plants in the United States convert corn and other grains into fuel. Gasoline suplemented with ethanol is available in more and more places every year.

We can all save oil by changing our lives a little bit, too. In nice weather, try riding your bike to school instead of getting a ride from Dad. The same is true for after-school soccer practice. And recycle those plastic bottles and bags. They're made from oil, too. Or try taking your own cloth bags to the grocery store; that way you'll never need the plastic bags at all.

Oil and oil products are used for many things. What are some other ways that you could conserve the oil that is left?

GLOSSARY

crude oil (krood oil) oil as comes from the ground before it has been refined

drill bit (dril bit) sharp part or cutting edge of a drill

energy (EN-er-jee) the power to do work

ethanol (ETH-uh-nawl) fuel made from corn stalks and other plant material

fossil fuel (FOS-uhl FYOO-uhl) hydrocarbon deposit, such as oil, made from living matter of ancient times and used for fuel

geologists (jee-OL-uh-jists) scientists who study the structure of the Earth

monopoly (muh-NOP-uh-lee) exclusive control by one group of the means of producing or selling a commodity or service

nonrenewable resource (non-ri-NOO-ey-buhl REE-sawrs) something that is useful that cannot easily be replaced

permeable (PUR-mee-uh-buhl) something that can be penetrated, especially by liquids or gases

petroleum (puh-TROH-lee-uhm) thick, flammable mixture of hydrocarbons that occurs naturally beneath the Earth's surface

refined (ri-FAHYND) made free of impurities

reserves (ree-SURVS) oil deposits still in the ground

FOR MORE INFORMATION

Books

Anderson, Laurie Halse. *Ticket to Saudi Arabia*.
Minneapolis, MN: Carolrhoda Books, Inc., 2004.

Berger, Melvin. *Oil Spill!*
New York: Harper Collins Children's Books, 1994.

Johnston, Joyce. *Alaska*. Minneapolis, MN: Lerner Publications, 2002.

Laughlin, Rosemary. *John D. Rockefeller: Oil Baron and Philanthropist*.
Greensboro, NC: Morgan Reynolds, Inc., 2004.

Other Media

Find out more about oil in the United States at *http://www.eia.
doe.gov/kids/energyfacts/sources/non-renewable/oil.html*

Find out more about all current sources of energy at *http://
www.hmns.org/generic/wiess_photo_captions.asp*

INDEX

Abu Dhabi, 24

blowouts, 21
Brazil, 27

California, 8
Canada, 8, 25
China, 6–7
crude oil, 10

Drake, Edwin, 7
drill bits, 17
drilling, 18–21

energy, 5
ethanol, 27–28
Exxon Valdez, 26

Fort McMurray, 25
Fossil fuels, 5
fuel-efficient vehicles, 27

gas stations, 10
geologists, 14–16

hybrid cars, 27

internal combustion engine, 8

Japan, 7

legal work associated with
   oil exploration, 19

Mexico, 8

monopoly, 9

Nigeria, 19
nonrenewable resource,
   5, 23, 27

oil
   composition of, 5–6,
      11–13
   drilling for, 18–21
   exploration for, 14–16
   history of, 6–10
   scarcity of, 23–24
   uses of, 4, 7–8, 27
oil derricks, 20
oil lamps, 7
oil shortages, 22
oil spills, 26
Oklahoma, 8

Pennsylvania, 7
permeable rocks, 12–13
petroleum, 12

refined oil, 8
reserves, 25
Rockefeller, John D., 8–9
Russia, 8

Saudi Arabia, 19
ships, 16, 26
Standard Oil, 8–10
Stanley Steamer, 8

tar sands, 25
Texas, 8
thumper trucks, 16

U.S. Supreme Court, 9

Venezuela, 19

ABOUT THE AUTHOR

Kathleen Manatt is a long-time writer, editor, and publisher of books for children. Many of her books have been about faraway places, which she likes to visit. She grew up in Illinois, Iowa, New Jersey, and California, and lived in Chicago for many years as an adult. She has climbed pyramids in Mexico, ridden elephants in Thailand, and toured the fjords of Norway. She has also visited Moscow, Lisbon, Paris, Geneva, London, Madrid, Edinburgh, and Barcelona. She now lives in Austin, Texas.

9/05